Us
&
Everything Else

Evocative Poetry

Françoise Hélène

London Royal Poetry Press

Françoise Hélène

www.francoisehelene.com
Instagram: francoisehelenepoetry
Illustrations by Mays Jasel

The beauty of poems is that you can let your imagination flow and let each poem understand your mind and the world around you. Poetry unifies humanity. Poems are therapeutic. They are part of our broken soul, our happiness, our dreams, our nightmares and everything in between. I hope you can find a piece of yourself within this book.
Even though each human is unique, we go through similar experiences and feel similar emotions.

Life is quite a ride. Turn each page from beginning to end to see the bigger picture.

With love,

Françoise Hélène

Françoise Hélène

Acknowledgements

Dear reader,

This is my first poetry collection and it is as raw as it can be.
Thank you for taking the time to read it and for your support.
I hope you can find a piece of yourself within my words.
I'm grateful you came across this book and I hope it brings you
love.

Thank you to the special people in my life who supports my wild-
est dreams. Thank you for believing in from the beginning.
I love you a lot for that.

Love,

Françoise Hélène

Contents

Françoise Hélène

The Author

Characters of different stories I let them be.

Tracing with a pencil the inner of my beauty
my flaws never appeared so perfectly.

When the sun awakens
this dysfunctional world sets me free.
And when it goes to sleep in its red and orange blankets
It takes me away in a surreal solitude,
It's my peace of mind.

When I find myself in darkness
I feel pain on the tip of my fingers.
The fear, the adrenaline make me feel more alive than ever.

This loneliness lives in my soul
I do not want it, yet I do need it.

If you tore it apart, It won't always get ruined.

The wind sounds like infinity
with pretty birds and flying wings
unfolding a lecture of its kind, of its meaning.

My rhythms are playing the piano;
they are the tranquillity I possess in me.

My reflection when I see it, it talks to me
I listen even if I don't always agree.

The unknown and uncertainty temporarily destroy me
still when another chapter finishes
I will always be, the narrator of this undefined story.

SUNRISE

We often rise at our highest when we have accepted who we are, but it's often a long journey to get there.

Françoise Hélène

A Mother's Kind of Love

She enters her home like she's slipping on ice.

She collides instantly in the crackle of her children's singing.
The end of the day exhausted her mind
yet there she is laughing
like it's early morning on a Saturday.
Showing the brave smile
of a woman who calmly embraces her priorities.
It's the way she holds them that will tell you her story
as she slightly pulls their shirt towards her heart
It's her present reality
In her touch, you can see
they give her a kind of love
the kind
she lives for.

For My Niece and Nephews

When the little people are around me
my worries don't stand a chance.
Funny laughs and cheeky smiles
when the little people tell a joke, the sun and rain reconcile
and a rainbow appears between the clouds.

Enchanting voices and pretty blue eyes
when the little people look at me
trouble stops growing in my garden and tulips rises.
Vast imagination and minds full of solutions
when the little people fear I am in danger
they send dragons to fly and conquer.

Small little jeans and jolly dresses
when the little people are with me
I always look my best.
Big genuine hearts and the sweetest touch
when the little people see my flaws
they always love me just as much.

Little people do not stay so little
someday, taller than me they'll be
but to me little people they will always be!

Françoise Hélène

Hopeless Romantic

I am fighting against the starry night to stay awake.
On my balcony, a bird left a red rose at sundown
and sang for the rain upon arrival
while my head was nonsense dreaming.

A book with blank pages,
black ink and a feather to write
were left at my front door.

Mind and heart awake
I am writing love letters to my soulmate
until the sun shines again.

Nightingales, singing in excitement for a new delivery
but perhaps, I am missing the home address.

Words of Love

Kiss my lips
like a bee kisses a flower.
Look at me
like a sailor craves the sea.
Touch me
the way leaves land in the wind.
Give me chills
like when snowflakes fall on my nose.
Warm me up
like the sun melts icebergs.
Make me feel
the way tears cry of joy.
Love me
like I love you.

Françoise Hélène

True Love

He was a stranger when our eyes met for the first time.
His soul was a new kind of love
one I have never felt.

His voice, musical
his language, lyrical,
he kissed me with his words.

He was somebody I could not explain
yet could fully understand.

Our souls were puzzle pieces that lost each other in the distance.
He felt like finding the unknown to my familiarity.

The pouring rain was the sun of our passion.
His breath around me was my highest ecstasy
with him, I lived in a world of solo beauty.

He undressed the layers of my soul
before he caressed my body.
He assured me I was capable with him
but could accomplish more on my own.

He was the wish I never wished for
because I did not believe someone else pieces could complement
the purpose of my existence so well.
He was the man I didn't need but wanted.

How lucky I am to have met a longing part of my soul I had been
missing.

Dancing at Sunset

A ballerina dancing in the dark
with delicate thoughts
holding the sunset at the tip of her fingers
singing her melody
as a bird announcing a new life
that's been born in its nest at twilight.

Stars falling around her
delivering brilliance,
turning it into elegance.
She is wearing a colour of innocence
a pastel pink dress so the clouds
can get lost in her skin
and dance through her heartbeats.

She is dancing in hope
faith
belief.

She is dancing for her own
selfless dreams.

Françoise Hélène

The Empty Drawer

Golden bracelets, diamonds and rare blue pearls.
Trending gadgets and sparkling shoes
Things I do not own
left languishing in the wooden drawer I do not have.
I am too busy walking in parks
admiring the city from afar
and mesmerising dancing trees.

The Island

I hear his silence across the sea of cries.
He is standing at the shore waving
at the sailing boat of his miscellaneous
unfinished forgiveness
spreading them in the white sand of his lover's trace.

Holding the best of each other at the bottom of their feet
silver rings at their tippy-toes
I hear a kind of voice that expresses a new sound.
Rising comfortably on the island
of Juliet roses and valley oak trees
they are blossoming
among everything that is breathing
through invented normality.

They are the survivors of the story of their ancestors
full of raw differences
I hope they know
they are a kind beauty.

Françoise Hélène

Childhood Story

You felt like you never fitted with the world's complexities
with its attitude
with its thoughts
its actions
its majority.

You cried yourself to sleep too many times trying to save yourself.
Then out of somewhere grew
an undercover strength from your heavy pain
your disappointments
your deceptions.

A strength that became stronger than your body
and settled in your mind.

And suddenly everything around you
started to fit in with you.

Us & Everything Else

The Enchanted Forest

If only all of us could have met in the same school backyard
at the same hour, next to the tree behind where we used to hide
because of unfaithful words
from people who thought they were something more than us.

We felt eternity when we couldn't stop crying
because we didn't know we were nothing less than them.
Though, we cannot forget each sorrow tree
represents a forest
full of loved Souls.

I didn't come into this world to fit in.

Françoise Hélène

Introverts and Extroverts

Show me different layers of who you are
as when a child discovers colors of the rainbow.

Let me open the door to your deepest treasures
by turning the keys to your secrets.

Let me take your breath
to a place where the air exhales your beauty.

Try to run and hide though my thoughts will travel your mind.

None can fool me
when I am the one who adores a heart of mystery.

Find me patiently waiting for your inner outsider.
Sense us free and let me see
the bird that's an acrobat
but refuses to fly.

Personalities

For Writers

A beautiful soul holding a restless, brilliant mind.
Pages of her story are a sweet work of art.
Her book cover is a goddess silhouette
that breathes on every bookshelf.

Literature connects humanity. Thank you, writers, for making this happen.

Françoise Hélène

I Hear Different

I love the way you hear
understand, listen to me.
Here we are
sitting in this small garden
where people come to play.
Here we meet
and beside your innocent smile
 could stay awake until dawn.

Here comes the sun
laying on our faces for some afternoon vitamin D.
Here go the drums
as one is slowly tapping his feet up and down on the grass.
Here comes the acoustic guitar
 as one is tickling the wind-chime that falls from an oak tree.
Here joins the piano
as one is flickering two sets of keys on a wooden bench
left, right, right to left.

Here goes the singer
as words of love and sorrow are moving upon her lips.
Here comes the violin solo
as one is trying to get rid of a loud lingering bee
above his left shoulder.
Here you are, now dancing
I can tell the beat of the music is rising.
Here comes the band carrying their instruments
and I am eager to feel the vibrations of music.
I've forgotten to tell you
I lost my hearing when I was five years old
though perhaps you understood this
from the beginning.

Music connects humanity. Thank you, musicians, for making this possible.

Side by Side

Our souls complement each other so well
they are identical
they're the polar opposite.

It's like we spent our lives
in parallel
in a distant world
growing like same-length orange trees
until we met with time
that's how you understand my heart
my soul
who I am
and who you are.

Friendship

Françoise Hélène

The Canvas

You are blank
you look a little pale
perhaps, you are exhausted.

Though in all truth you cannot feel
any emotions.
Your body is a sharp shape
you are framed with ambiguity
you are standing on three legs
beside a French window
that lets you see, nature you could become.

I am drawing grass on your feet
I am making marks of lilies on your ankles
I am gently placing oak trees on your legs
I am letting kingfishers fly on your torso
I am weighing the sunset on your shoulders
I am leaving the moon on your neck
I am delicately throwing a splash
of heart gradient at your head.

You are a paint brush's best lover
a colour's best explanation
you are images to silent words.

You are the blank emotions need
to express themselves.

You are therapeutic for the mind
you are the beginning of a story
waiting to be told.

The arts connect humanity. The beauty of universal language. Thank you, artists, for creating this.

For the Ones Who Feels Misunderstood

The girl with the unspoken smile
dreams in silence
and observes the scene from far.

She sings in the background
as her voice tries to surrender.

Lights are getting darker on the screen of life
and the excited unknown.
She is misunderstood,
piece by piece
as her reality unfolds,
will someone notice through her eyes
the flesh of her heart and where she holds it
when life gets hard.

She holds modesty so well
tucked in the bottom of her feet
while the world around her
screams novelty.

Françoise Hélène

The Traveller

In a suitcase inside where she packed her life away
for another everything new
where her heart has already landed
yet nothing as concrete as the soil of her feet.

She sees the hidden beauty in the world
with an infinite vision, she created for herself.

She carries her house in her body
and wherever she lands her unknown surroundings
become her backyard
where she keeps her garden of flowers.

She's the one making each city bloom
with her travelling soul
the whole world is her home.

Old Souls

I see clouds throughout North.
I've left my compass at home on purpose.
I am hugging a tree and dancing along with its leaves.
I follow a trace of my ancestors.
I was here once before.
Here,
is where I was always going to return.

Françoise Hélène

For the Child in You

You little star that shines so bright
you make the whole sky look glorious
from a million miles away.

RAINY DAYS

I was doing so well and carried my emotions in my head,
until now where they burst out of my heart
and dropped all over me.

The beauty of being human and life experiences; feeling emotions. I hope you can relate to at least one of the following poems, and that they lead you to self-reflection.

Françoise Hélène

About a Time

Tell me about a time you came home and cried
because you had a bad day and let me tell you about mine too.

My Day *(for the times I felt sad)*

The world fell on me today.
I failed for the hundredth time.
My weakness is all that's left of me
I hold my broken hopes and dreams in the scars of my mistakes.

I shower and let teardrops wash away the chills on my skin.
I feel crazy
I feel insane
I lose a piece of my humanity.
I explode with rage and disappointment.
I am furious
I am the thunder.

What do I do when I feel like nothing is left of me?
I live rock bottom as long as I need to
I pierce time in forever
and start building a new strength
for the hundred and first time.

Françoise Hélène

The Slow Dance

I am slow dancing with the world
for the first time in centuries.
I am following its footsteps and moving in the distance
while its rhythm falls in the background.

Its music is playing notes of fear in a gentle tone
It's singing in a high-pitched voice of hope.

A story that began with a draining melody
then continued with one that replenished my soul.
I am losing myself in this moment
from sunset to sunrise over and over again
in this newly abandoned ballroom
that led me to a full stage with an empty audience.

Who knew dancing with my inner world
could feel so beautiful.

Do you make time for yourself?

Beauty of The Earth

The world fell apart and united
the morning trees burned the sun
to spread dust over the highest mountains
instead of mid-March snow.

In a place where the voice of our silence spoke
to replace existing sounds
side by side million souls are having the loudest conversations.

In the presence of a dysfunctional reality
slightly drowning in the broadest spread of fear
I begged the rain in my tears to calm down
instead of trying to swim my way up
afraid to lose something so pure and natural
my breath.

Breathing moments day by day
the moonlight is keeping me blind in the awakened night.

The clouds keep leaking
between the cracks of my open windows
to give me a little more of the earth
while I step back and let it take the lead.
I watch it bloom
I let it be, wide-open
without me.
I give it time to grow
as it's been suffocating for too long.
I settle for uncertainty
in the hope my insanity will demolish this sinking hole.
I embrace my flaws
and let them become the inspiration of my future
and pre-formed disaster
where the purest of beauty creates itself.

Françoise Hélène

In the Studio

I am dancing to the beat of my white high heels
on an ancient wooden floor
in an old art studio
where bright windows were abandoned
now waiting to talk to sunlight and night skies.

I see your lips starring at me
while my well-shaped body and satin skin
shows you the meaning of sensuality.

I am moving along with your shadow.
Your eyes alowly peeling my red dress off my body.
Come closer, let my heart whisper
to your inner doubts
the questions to your answers.

Leave your arrogance behind the curtains.
Shut the doubtful door
come with your raw self
for once
to this place you love more than you can admit.

Then maybe we could do more
than just dancing.

That September

When we danced in the fall
under the coloured leaves umbrellas
by the sunset shy hands interlaced their fingers.
You looked at me and said I looked like the heart of September.
Left a trace of your lips on my forehead
until you drew your kiss through me
so I couldn't see how dearly you adored me.
Behind the autumn words
sang the songbird for a new season.
An unfinished story in the book of our adventure
began in the hard-cold November
a melody awaits
and swallows our deepest worries
as we can't keep our eyes off each other.

Françoise Hélène

You And I

Don't ask me to choose between
the rain and the sun
snow and grass
love or Infatuation
madness or decency.

I'd love to feel them all
between the walls of you and me.

The Swings

Remember twenty-five years ago
when we were sitting on the swings in my backyard,
we were four years old.
I threw my sandals in the summer air
you picked them up
slid my feet back in them
and told me I was your Cinderella.
You promised me when we'd be old enough
you'd marry me one day.

I wish you would have kept that promise.

Françoise Hélène

The Beginning

We were talking in the cold night.
He leaned over, his lips touched mine
for the very first time.
It's not that I was drowning in his sensuality
it was that no one ever kissed my heart.

It could have meant nothing but it felt
like I knew him from thousands of lifetimes before.
Now I know
it was the beginning of everything we'd ever have.

What If?

How can I be certain if I am making the right decision
when I have doubts about almost everything that comes with it?

If a fire can burn a sea
is it an illusion
or have I always understood it all wrong?

Until the moment I drain the sand from my eyes
by looking down at the sun
while dropping stressed heartbeats
on the moving ground
If time stands still
should I stay here for as long as I can
out of fear of finding myself broken, instead of content?

If I am left wondering
is it worse than finding myself borderline
on a new chaotic reality?
If I risk it all, and get through the danger,
through sufferings and overcome barriers
will it lead me to the better?

If I survive it all better than I imagined
with my underlying courage
have I created the impossible for myself?

If a fish can drown
and birds can never stop flying
was all of it ever real?

Françoise Hélène

Healing

I didn't recognise it at first
the process of falling all at once
from a balcony as high as birds can fly.

The inside of my feet is bleeding
while I am walking on stones.

It feels like a wooden log lit up in the fireplace
an unspoken promise
left languishing in a drawer somewhere.

It feels like a part of me has been left behind
to meet my present self
and marry my future me.

It feels like breaking
finding
being
surviving
becoming,
it feels like healing.

Sapphire

Ocean space cannot teach us how to swim.
Still an old boat could get repaired and make it across,
someday,
even if it's still half-broken.

The sea once searched for a storm
the sky accepted its proposition
by making it as dry as a desert.

We are left with nothing.

We are lost in this adventure
it's you and me, do we care to wonder?

I don't need much of anything
as long as you stay with me
so I can dive into your eyes made of sapphire
and find a piece of my own shelter.

Françoise Hélène

Broken Love

Our artificial love broke many times
we tried repairing it
but after a while it had no effec,t
it had no use.

The River

In the autumn wind my heart fell behind a tree
near the river.
Where we fed long-lasting drops of love
to floating sorrows
and swans.

His eyes were as sweet as he seemed
he left my hands bare through the sudden thunder.

I thought he'd cry of loneliness in the night
though the storm was watching over him.

A gentle sound, a clear blue sky
awakened in the morning
it was all he needed to fly away
leaving only a feather to stay.

Françoise Hélène

Temporary

When we lose a piece of love
we were holding so close
to our heart
and our soul
for so long.

We sometimes wonder
if it will return
the same or differently
or if it has it fallen beneath
the settling of our past.

Identity

Have we fought against each other's rights
or against our misunderstood, and broken identities?

Françoise Hélène

The New Home

Cold ice wind breaking through my skin to my bare bones
the winter often loves to pour rain on my naked shoulders
during times of war.

Where I live satisfaction comes
from finding knowledge on the route to empty treasures.

"Come to my castle" whispered in my ears a mighty
fast horse, "I will take you dancing by the river
and away from your solitude."
"Trust me to find the way after moonlight hour, close your eyes
and prepare yourself for a delightful surprise."

I sink into what my heart can see, eyes full of sincere innocence.
How will I retrace my footsteps
if I dislike the place upon arrival?
A second to decide
the forest is dark and deep and we're on our way.
I fell asleep through the galloping
the yellow of the sun, woke me late morning.
Finding myself in a medieval-style room
and it's as sweet as pancakes and maple syrup for breakfast.

Us & Everything Else

Thinking of You

(for every time I think of you)

I hear the features of your face
tap dancing in my eyes' pocket
on repeat.

Françoise Hélène

Record Player

(for the times I needed music to surrender)

The rhythm of your song
falls in reverse in my old record player
where the storm of my thoughts
overwhelmed by your nature
hits me to the ground
and mutes the voice of the enchanted bluebird's cry.

Defending his harmonies
with what's left of the morning sun
exploding in a silent melody
a defeating heart somewhere
won the battle of its own production.

Voice

It terrifies me, how you pretend to be so kind to me
when I can hear your thoughts speak to me
instead of your voice.

Françoise Hélène

What Do You Think?

Is it the obstacles that stop us from blossoming
among our scariest worries
or is it the fears themselves?

The Train

(for the times I didn't felt listened to)

You taught me how to build walls
so I could protect myself
and build a house where I could stay
in the same comfort of everyday life.

Yet what I wanted was to learn how to build a train so,
I could get away and live
comfortably in all other places.

Françoise Hélène

Kiss-In-The-Dark-Street

I met him on Kiss-in-the-dark street
a place beside my age fourteen's bedroom door.
A time when he became my forbidden
escape to love.
I understood a few years later
the smell of his aura never described
the intentions of his perfum so well.

His lips tasted like fire on ice
and he ran after he melted my heart.

My height was never the same since.

(learning from a broken heart)

Lions and Buffalos

(for the times I wondered if and how I could ever inspire the world)

I have dreamt of a better place
where fireworks and thunder share
brightness among the stars.

Where lions and buffalos embrace
each other in sleepless nights.

Where truth and lies confide in each other.

Where courage always takes over fear.
And where better places exist
not only in dreams.

Françoise Hélène

Can I

(for the times I believed in the impossible)

Can I go back behind the curtains to hide from ghosts
until I become one myself?

Can I save the ones who suffer from starvation
by flying to all and give them the feeling of being full?

Can I carry the moon
to give light to the darkest stars?

Can I free the extinct
by feeding them hope in reproduction?

Can I cure the out of breath
by changing their lungs to air?

Can I exchange the worst
for something wonderful?

Even if I don't know how?

Your Resonance

(for the times someone long-forgotten crossed my mind)

When the clouds reach the mountains
and my forest hides in silence,
that's when I'll remember your resonance.

Françoise Hélène

Falling
(for the times I felt melancholy)

Fear of loss when everything falls upon us
and crushes a bit of our soul, deep in our veins
where broken hopes live.

How do I find my strength
beneath endless layers of horrifying thoughts?

Shadow

I looked elsewhere and walked across the full crowds,
I found similar to you.
They carried your shadow
behind the empty sun
they made me wonder
if they also carried your soul
but in this world it seems,
you are one of a kind.

Françoise Hélène

Sleepless

Don't mind me
if I look at the ground today.
My eyes are carrying the tears
that kept the night awake.

Love

I am happy, by myself
with friends and family
and the people I have in my life.
But sometimes
I wish I could hold a love
that could set my soul on fire
by lighting up the flames of lust
that makes the inside of me burn for love.

Françoise Hélène

The Mask

It feels like I walked to work naked this morning
even though I am wearing clothes and make-up.
Nothing can cover the dark emotions
I feel inside from this evil world temporarily living in me.
Yet, here I am
opening the office door
putting on my brightest shoes
and dressing myself with a smile.

Set Free

When you left, you set me free of pain.
A pain I didn't know I carried in me,
until then.

Françoise Hélène

White Hydrangeas

(for the times I worked hard and failed)

I planted seeds to grow white hydrangeas
but all that grew were dead trees
that touched the sky at thunder.

One Day

Sometimes we are so hurt
so in pain
so in love
that we don't understand the way we act.

We are afraid,
so we destroy and move away
from everything we ever wanted
because it's terrifying to think
we could lose it all, one day.

Françoise Hélène

The Lake

(for the times I overcame challenges)

It's a midnight chance
stumbling on the edge of a black water lake.
Risky flies surrounding your wounds
the navy sky speaks to you gently.
Dirt bike roads afraid of swimming holes
drops of sorrow
falling on the flesh of your grace.

Let it all embrace you
until you wake up in the morning,
empty and renewed.
Ready for a new beginning
and allow yourself to admire the birds land
on the golden lake.

Ghosting

You left my head thinking about the memories
we could have built in the house of our future wonders.

Françoise Hélène

The Note

I saw your picture in a note from my memory.
I knew we hadn't spoken for a while
though I didn't realise how long it had been
since we touched skin to skin
since we kissed lips to lips
since we spoke heart to heart
since we looked eye to eye.

I cannot remember when we stopped.
Perhaps none of it ever began.

Norms

(for the times I questioned the mainstream)

Can I doubt the shape of the earth?

Can I judge a minute for lasting sixty seconds,
a day for being grey or cold
and leaves for falling from trees?

Can I speak too loud when I am angry
or stay quiet when I disagree?

Can I forget about the norms
and make some of my own?

Françoise Hélène

The Universe

Can freedom be the wind?
Can the sun have a soul's hope?
Can trees watch upon my pain?
Can planets empty my sorrow?
Can the stars find my strength when it's lost?

Can the earth be our feelings?

Broken Spell

He caught me by surprise on a quiet night
when I went searching for the moon
that was missing from the sky.

His footsteps were the song of broken dry leaves.

He is no mystery when all he makes me feel is contagious fear
about us and the rest of the world.

He was holding his heart in his hands
offering nothing less than his loyalty.

A broken spell
I refused for it to exist.

His eyes full of sorrow drowning
in loneliness.

How can I give him a piece of my happiness
when all I have to offer is my absence?

All I could do was walk away in a timeless uncertainty
hoping he'd be brave enough to follow.

Françoise Hélène

STORMS

What I love the most about storms is who I've become and how I feel once I've overcome them.

(my darkest emotions)

Hero

Once in a while, he allowed himself to get away from this non-sense and craziness that was surrounding him.

When he looked at me, I saw my reflection through his eyes, for a moment, I felt like a meaningless love poem, written on a wrinkled piece of paper thrown in a high, satisfying burning fire.

Holding his sweaty hand, I could feel the pain with him, even if he didn't want me to.

Kicking the evil dust falling at his feet, pushing away the demons that were heavily crashing on him.

Surviving every obstacle of mortality, bleeding and destroying his own hands by climbing the tallest mountain of victory.

With every deception and unexpected distress, his strength was more powerful than he'd ever know.

For a moment I could see his stories in my head, bombarding my imagination with pictures I was hoping I'd never see.

Wasting drops of his sanity in a timeless rush of eternity.

Stuck somewhere between non-existent normality and twisted insanity. He lived in a world of his secrecy.

Embracing every defeat, attacking my soul with bravery.

He is the heart of my rescue.

He is my hero.

Françoise Hélène

The Tunnel

Our mind is made of puzzled conflicts,
and when we manage to put them together,
the turbulence creates our own and unique masterpiece.
We juggle with our life dangers and we jump through the roof of
an unsettled house the moment we choose our final decision.
In the underground corridor, we can hear the sound of the dead
lizard skin tear apart and the beating heart of the stolen swan.
We fight for the unusual and, we let our weaknesses take us away
in the tunnel of darkness on our brightest days.
In the distance, we can see vibrations of rumbling echoes,
rolling on the ceramic floor of this "no stops" road.
We walk along, and our legs become heavy with fatigue.
Passing and slowly moving beside the singer with no voice,
we admire the song of his silence.
We feel the sea trembling under our feet, and we let the pressure
push us down between the fictional walls, we built for ourselves.
In the broken mirror we left behind years ago,
we look deep in our eyes,
and we try to find the escape of the black angel wings we buried
in our soul.
We cross the paths we choose to cross,
we let the traffic pass ahead of us and then, we stop.
Completely.
And suddenly, unexpectedly, the flames inside of us stop burning.
The water went over the bridges and we surf through each wave
of trust with confidence.
We get up We don't look back.
We start over and then, we never start again.

Lost Love

A lost love,
travelling far away in a hidden world.
Buried under a dark and invisible soul blanket.
Drifting away slowly in time,
It will never be found.
An unspoken melody playing loudly in the background of life.
Broken records,
playing every note perfectly.
A high-pitched voice,
screaming and singing endearingly.
An open black book,
covered with dust,
left lonely for years on a forgotten shelf in a lively house.
An unwritten story that's been read how it was supposed to be.
Burning candles,
outside in the wind spreading the smell of mystery
under the half-moon from the morning sun that never rose.
Easy riddles with unrevealed answers,
complicated intentions wondering above their understanding.
Beliefs of hopes that were led by the truth,
leading the misleading of this unsolved hazard.
Unreal chances ran out too quickly
by doing a favour and eliminating possibilities.
A misfortune that's never been so lucky,
feeling such a significant intensity from an unexplained curiosity.
White transparent curtain closing the door
to an unwelcome generosity.
Reckless games with structured rules and undefined winners.
Wrong decisions, finished by happy endings.
A lost love that meant everything and forever nothing.

Françoise Hélène

Eggshell

Cracking the hard eggshell on my sharpest kitchen glass was like seeing my heartbreak in front of me.

How can you open me up and let the liquid of my blood disperse so softly?

How did you manage to rip a piece of my heart when I was still alive?

And walk away with it,

without giving it back to me.

Infinitely

I was there with you in that moment.
I wanted it to last until I no longer existed
until the end of me in years time.
I soaked my spirit in your clear water
and nailed my fingers to your ground.
My heart is yours infinitely.

It killed me to say goodbye to you.
Yet, the most painful part
was that I was still alive.

Françoise Hélène

THE LESSONS

This chapter is going to be different.
Completely different.

You will grow.
You will show the world
the authentic you by loving yourself.

You will let the right people go
to welcome your soul tribe.
You'll make space for what aligns
with your truest self.
Abandon
of what served you wrong
and forgive yourself for past mistakes.

It won't always be easy
but it will be okay.
The best parts of yourself
are about to blossom.
Are you ready?

Pain Makes You Stronger

You grow stronger after heartbreak
like the pouring rain nourishes trees,
flowers,
the earth,
instead of making them drown.
Like painful tears
make your heart stronger
after every drop.

Françoise Hélène

Positivity

I said
"We better head home, the storm caught the rage, and this tree
will soon split in two."
He said,
"Look at the beauty of the descending rain, the trees are dancing
in the wind. I want to glue my feet to the earth and dance with it."

Sprinkle of Hope

When I lost hope,
hope came and found me,
when I stopped believing in faith,
faith believed in me.

Françoise Hélène

Number One

I wanted you forever
until forever became a clock.
I meant every word I said to you
but then I lost myself in contradictions.
I wanted the pages of our story to keep turning
but I ran out of pencils to write.
I loved the us we built
but then I started making myself.
I didn't want to give up
until I gave too much.
I intended to paint our future
but I could only draw our past.
I was moving forward
until I took a step back and turned right instead of wrong.
I wanted it to be us until the end
but then I started putting myself first.
That's when I became my everything,
that's when I started loving myself.

Expectations

Dark empty night,
calm and peaceful drops of rain tapping on my open window.
The fresh smell of adventure and hope,
moonlight shining bright.
I am falling asleep to the sound of the singing wolf.

Captivating,
endearing dreams,
small bats flying in full circles.
We can't fight against the whole world
it's cynical.

Warm summer breeze,
the near distance shows me the knowledge of the sea.
I lit a fire next to some rocks,
the flames burn the rain
as they kiss and touch.
I am mesmerised and shocked,
at how fulfilling this night turned out to be.

Françoise Hélène

Personal Growth

The sound of the rain on a beautiful day,
screaming for my heart to erase the pain in my chest.
I am no longer desperate for what I know I deserve.
I no longer need to prove myself to others
when I've already declared my worth
to who I am.
I dance with the storm
knowing it will finish when the time is right.
Yet until the calm hits the ground
I will listen to my thunder,
bloom and grow
with every piece I am.

Letting Go

I observe the sunset hypnotising
me in the unknown,
In the sense of upcoming,
uplifting adventures
leaving me at the beginning
of a wonderful journey
that's surrounded by beauty.

A moody sky that burns meaningless relationships.
A soulful wind that invites trustworthy ones
to replace grief with solid comfort.

No goodbye is ever easy
yet they do feel right sometimes
and that is all there is to them.

Françoise Hélène

Mutual Support

I met you in time in the heart of my favourite beauty of yours.
You let me breathe your faith as deep in my lungs,
as far as I could.

My endless anxiety dissolved in the caves of my blood,
widespread despair has now gone
in the pocket of my past sorrows.

Because of you,
I will bury the worries from the strength I have built.
I am ending the agony that used to live within me.

I felt your tenderness diminish the inflammation of my pain.
You,
living
and surrounding me,
is you,
invading my soul with truthful aspirations.

You made me believe in what I thought had no chance.
I embrace the gold in you,
knowing we will never lose each other
because together, we are home.

Appreciating Differences

How can I be
so
into
your
record
when you're not my type of music?

Françoise Hélène

Awaken

You touched a piece of my soul with your mind.
A piece I didn't know my body carried,
the one that makes me feel alive the most.

Authenticity

One of the most incredible feelings
is feeling at home
through places,
people,
within yourself,
and who you are.

Françoise Hélène

Being Strong

I feel broken,
I am the glue to my bud vase
which crashed on my ceramic floor
when I hit it out of anger.
I try to hold my pride
on top of my head.
I am lost in a vulnerable place
I am fragile
I am already broken
though I am doing my best
to glue me back together.

Giving to Yourself

You gave me a sense of peace
I thought I never deserved to give myself.

Françoise Hélène

Self-Worth

I hope you know,
you are worth so much more,
than they ever made you feel.

Pieces

I admire your broken pieces and how strong you became.
I appreciate your perfections and imperfections.
I love the authenticity that makes you
everything you are.

Françoise Hélène

A Reply to The Poem "Pieces"

You made my non-existent perfect fall apart
and unfold gently in the arms of your pure acceptance.
Imperfections that became alive,
than anything that's ever been known as beautiful.

To Allow Space When Needed

We broke and stalled for a while
like a caravan stuck in the mud.
But we found each other again
somewhere between the rain
and we haven't stopped driving since.

Françoise Hélène

Self-Acceptance

I looked at her closely
and found something in her I've never seen before.
This time, she was stronger.
She fought and was a survivor.
The spark in her eyes
she was herself the new lover.
She was ready to conquer the world
with elegance and intelligence.
I looked at her one last time
and kissed her smile.

 "I am ready to keep blooming"
I told myself as I walked away
from the mirror.

Read this to yourself. Her/she/him/he

To Drop the Ego

Back to when we first met,
I was afraid of how you made me feel,
because it was like nothing I felt before.
Stupefaction showered me with silence,
and nonsense talking,
but your regard,
went straight to my soul.

Françoise Hélène

Growing Separately

You walked into my life unexpectedly.
The day I was carrying mountains,
on the back of my self-love.
To transform into something
more beautiful than there ever was.
You were the present that fitted into my future,
the long-lasting love that came to stay.

The Transition

I am in transition between
who I was
who I am
who I want to become
what I left behind
and where I am looking ahead.

Françoise Hélène

Believing

I felt a new rhythm coming through me.
The earth moving on my behalf,
in my favour.
It's closing the doors in the basement
of my second doubts
drilling patterns to lead me where I want to head to.
It's not a single road
nor a plan I once wrote on a map
it was engraved in the stars long ago
it's my destiny.

Doing What You Love

When the passion inside of you always burns for more
that's how you know, not only it is part of you
but you were meant to be part of it.

Françoise Hélène

Changes

An old flame once dusted by the wind
rising unexpectedly
in the enchanted forest.
Not making it burn this time
but making it grow.

Accepting Flaws

My loneliness envies company.
I searched for it for years,
a specific kind of love.
We all dream of something perfect
though could find something so much more beautiful.

Françoise Hélène

Old Stories

When I thought I lost everything,
all I lost were old stories,
the ones that didn't belong within me anymore.
Perhaps, it wasn't that I lost anything,
It's that I was getting rid of what was no longer right for me.

Moving at Your Own Pace

I am dancing to the songs
I wrote for myself
on the notes
that make me feel good.

Françoise Hélène

Have You?

Have you ever felt as you had everything
all the love in the world
when you were completely alone
and only had yourself?

To Trust Yourself

When the dust settled in the forest alongside naked trees
where leaves danced to find their way to the ground.
Through the weighted rain, a new day arises
with the darkest clouds.
The intangible awaiting
the arrival of touch.
We may dream until we surrender at dawn
and awake the impossible.

Françoise Hélène

Who Would You Send This Poem To?

You taught me how to be kind,
generous,
honest,
truthful,
trustworthy,
authentic,
by simply being yourself.

Taking Responsibility

People wondered about you.
About the way you are,
your actions,
the road you chose,
what you see ahead.

You're the only one who knows where you are heading to
and that is more than enough.

Françoise Hélène

To Embrace your Worth

I knew the kind of man I was hoping to meet
and be with but I didn't realise you equally hoped
finding someone like me,
too.

Generosity

Your toes were frozen from the winter storm
that kept you awake all night.
Your stomach left hungry from an apple dinner.
You understood what it meant to have less
than you should have had.
Then suddenly grew the money tree you planted
from the seeds of yourself
with your scarred hands.

You grew with it all.
Kept your kindness
and shared your gold with the ones
who used to live like you.

Françoise Hélène

Reward Yourself

I worked hard,
day after day,
evening upon evening,
trying to impress others
I'd forgotten i impressed myself.

Values

I thought about leaving because of our differences,
but I loved the way you lived your life,
and that was enough to make me fall in love.

Françoise Hélène

Finding Yourself

Though I kept missing you every day
I missed myself more when I wasn't alone
and finding my soul again
was the most beautiful feeling I've ever felt.

People You Trust

I love how I can tell you the things I used to tell no one, not even myself. .

Françoise Hélène

"Knowing" in Yourself

Know,
you can succeed.
Not only can your success turn out well
but you can excel in it too.

Respecting Your Desires

I wanted to want you
but my mind was as stubborn as my heart
and I couldn't change the thinking of my desire.

Françoise Hélène

As Simple as That

How can you tell me what I like,
what I don't,
who I am,
when you are someone else.

SHORT STORIES

I haven't written since yesterday and my soul is screaming for a pen to fill blank pages.

Françoise Hélène

Where did all the superheroes go?

I remember.

In the heart of winter, watching the snow from my bedroom window, an evening sky upon the horizon and the smell of the last piece of wood, burning down to the last drop in the comfort of the mesmerising fireplace. Snowflakes were the size of my palm, and they were racing between each other to the finish line on the snow-covered slides in the half-empty park. I could climb all the slides from downwards to upwards. It made me feel strong, powerful, invisible, a little bit like Batman (because I had seen him in a film a week before and I know that's how he felt every time he won a battle against the bad guys, especially the Joker, who's far from being funny).

§

At six years old, I was scared during the nights, all too often, afraid of the moon monsters who always tried to sleep on my ceiling, next to my bright green shining stars. I thought they were just part of my nightmares, but I knew they liked hiding somewhere underneath my bed and would sneak their way out by climbing the walls like spiders (of whom I was never afraid). My brother read me stories about the moon monsters; they are too bright and stop you from sleeping! But the stars were always on my side and kept calling Spiderman who brought the dark to cover the moon monsters, so that I couldn't see them, and I could get back to sleep and have sweet dreams.

On a sunny day, back in the blossoming garden of my eleventh summer, I wanted to fly like Supergirl. I could live in my dreams after all. I ran as fast as I could for three minutes, about a thousand times, and I'd open up my arms, jump on the trampoline and try to fly, but it only ever left me face down in the grass. I told myself, "When I grow up and I am as old as her, I'll be able to fly and save the world." I just had to grow a few more inches in height, that was all.

§

My mum once told me at fifteen years old that I was still a kid. "I am not! I am so mature," I once snapped with a dedicated frustration. I wanted to prove this to her by getting my first job, as a babysitter for my neighbour's six and seven year old kids. I also insisted I'd walk to the closest shop, and I went shopping for my clothes.

There was one Sunday evening, when she let me have a sip of wine from her ruby-filled glass at dinner; I didn't like it.

Back then, people in their thirties seemed much older to me, but thought they were so young. Most were married, with a soon-to-be-pregnant wife. In a small village like mine, most people already knew each other, but I couldn't wait to meet my guy, the one that would kiss me upside down like Spiderman and let me live the love story I'd been waiting for all my life. I knew he was out there and would come along at the right time. A soft spot for a Spiderman, left no room for most-wanted Iron Man, indeed.

I am twenty-five and heartbroken for the third time and could not sleep last night because I had had a bad day at work. I am scared I'll never find the one. I want to sleep all night until morning and stop overthinking.

About everything.

Where did all the superheroes go?

Françoise Hélène

She Left

We were running between tall grass as if we were children playing in a bouncy house at a birthday party. Behind the house where she grew up in a small part of the world, we sat barefoot on a midhigh hill and watched the stars for hours, because I wanted to. Sharing stories about ourselves we'd both always been afraid to tell anyone else, I look at her and she makes me smile.
It's simple.
Her eyes are as brown as hazelnut and her golden sun-rained skin glimmered. It's a forbidden love because my heart has been hurt many times before and I couldn't open up the door to a future with her.
Like the ones who broke my love before, slowly, little by little when I suddenly heard silence, disappearance or the sound of another man's name whispering to my heart I should have been him.
She, SHE LEFT
Me feeling incredible and amazing
Over and over again
With all my flaws,
The deepest part of my soul
With all I am.
The rain dropped on us; it was our passionate connection. On a dark and cold autumn night all I had were her arms to comfort me and make me feel at home.
It was enough.
She is enough.
When I was far away from my past, drowning in the present and fearing my future.
I felt her love for me through her eyes. Her capturing my lips as she kissed my worries away. I do not doubt who I am with her or if I can live without her; I do not want to.
She's not what I'd always hoped for; she's better and not exactly what I could ever think about.

She and I, drowning in a world of inner beauty, of faulty accept-
ance, messed up moments, connecting souls, forgiveness and
unconditional love.
The waves of drama-free, insanity, pure, rare and hard-to-findkind
of love.
She made me believe long-lasting love is even more real
than my own existence.
I believe it for the very first time.
She's incredible.
But so am I.

Françoise Hélène

Behind the Mountains

Back in December, a few years ago, we sat here on this
half-broken wooden bench, not worried if it would fall apart or
not. A hot chocolate picnic to warm up our blood and a look at the
snow sprinkled mountains ahead of us, if I could only move them
a little to the right to make space for a few more trees alongside,
as there used to be.

Although I haven't forgotten the look of your eyes when they
make me feel at home, I have grown since, not a single inch more
but instead from my high-pitched voice to a bolder one.

I do not speak of what the world wants me to talk about; I do not
adapt or steal the sound of its voice anymore.

I let my words fall upon my lips for what I want to say
and I store in silence
what I don't want anyone else to hear from me.

I could choose to listen again and again when the noise explodes
through brick walls, but I do so only once, and I let go.

I walk away and try as hard as I can to care more about what I
think of myself than what others think of me, modestly,
sometimes.

But aren't we all pretending to be completely perfect for at least
an hour or six once in a while?

Haven't we all felt as if we had to hide our broken pieces in the
basement of our feet? Or are we that much different and can't
agree on more than a million things?

I create my everything and nothing, a place where it means the
same to have it all and not to have a single thing I want.

I'm a bit terrified of soaking my feet in the wrong puddle but the
water often dries on my skin and clothes after some time.

I walk with grace when I can in my sinking mistakes.

I've stumbled along the way but I see ahead on the top of these
mountains that I'll make it there when the time is right.

You taught me how to climb by giving me the right tools and by
expressing my silent thoughts.

And you taught me how to build strength through my bare bones
by lifting weights of courage.
Just when I was about to fight against the contradictions of my
misconceptions.
The only side you took was ours,
over and over again.
Feather and son,
far away in the same little world.
Count me in your team
until I can build a train and road from the Swiss Alps
to the middle of the stormy sky.

Françoise Hélène

The Outfit

There is a closet in my room, holding an outfit I'm not ready to wear, yet. It's my favourite colour, a colour most of my friends don't seem to choose too often, as a first choice. My parents placed it on a shelf I couldn't reach. Yet.

It's similar to a uniform, wanting to keep itself safe, for a hobby I'm not yet ready to take part in, until I find the right team.

I loved my wooden desk, placed in the corner of my room by the most significant window. All I could see was a piece of a brick wall from the neighbours' house. Throughout the school years, Mum and Dad watched me from afar, when I was drawing on blank pages that became filled with myself and everything I loved, when I left my bedroom door slightly opened on quiet evenings at home. Their eyes told me each morning; I, their only child, wasn't ready to face reality. Yet.

The mirror was my enemy for decades; it always reminded me of the shape of my body, what it looked like and what it held.

What was it missing?

What was too much?

Years of struggling, of hiding and showing the world myself, from my eccentric attitude to my different clothing style; "I am trapped in a cage, a cage that lives inside of me." was a constant thought of mine. My body.

I wanted it to change.

I wanted to make it my own.

I tried to find my ladder of confidence for a long time but all I could see was how rusty it was.

I was terrified of climbing higher.

"What will they think of me?" I thought a thousand times.

Then came the day the outfit unfold in my arms and I put it on, along with my best accessories.

Myself. I. Am. Beautiful.

That's when I realised I never needed a ladder

Because there were steps to learn beforehand all along.

My mirror became my best friend!

Marshmallows in 2020

I remember that one evening so clearly.

It was a beautiful evening and the children had played in the garden of the cottage most of the day. It was one of these nights we were going to have a campfire, with marshmallows and a triple chocolate homemade dip the kids had made with their daddy that morning. It's still Noah's favourite, after all these years. He had turned eight that summer.

It was August, his favourite month of the year. "Could we have an August in the winter?" he once asked, deadly serious. He loved the winter snow and skating, but summers in Canada are mostly warm and sunny, and he used to adore swimming in the sea and camping trips. He still does.

The stars were brighter than usual that night, as was the full moon, shining through the starry sky. Emily was trying to tickle her brother, and asked him for a cuddle. He laughed; she put her arms around him and kissed him on his left cheek. He then ran inside with his father to watch a film.

The wind was getting slightly colder when Emily asked in a tired tone, "Mummy, why didn't we go see Grandma?" I embraced her. "Well my darling, there's a new virus called coronavirus travelling throughout the world, and a lot of people in the world are working together to understand the virus, so that we can protect ourselves from it. Many of us need to stay near our home and keep our distance at this time to stop the virus from spreading. Many wonderful nurses and doctors, who we are grateful for, are working very hard and taking good care of the people who got unwell because of the virus, as it can affect each person differently." I remember thinking she was attentive, so I continued: "Grandma needs to rest now and lives an hour's flight away, but don't you worry. We'll be able to go back to her house and see her" She nodded, like a seven-year-old who proudly understood. "Okay. And even Uncle Felix who lives on the other side of the ocean, as you showed me on the map? Is he staying mostly near his home right now?"

"Yes darling, he's at home, in England," I replied.

The look on her face was priceless, before she added: "Should most people work together? Do we have to work with people we get along with less than others?" Surprised by her question, I replied: "Well, it depends. Sometimes we do but not always. It's best to work alongside people who encourage and support us, if possible."

"And what if I'm mad at the dog, Bubu, that made me drop my ice cream on the grass the other day? Does it mean I still have to say hello to him, next time I see him?" she asked.

"It would be very kind if you did, but that's for you to decide. If you are kind to others because you want to be, it also means you are brave, and a lot of great things often come out of brave kindness," I said. She kept talking: "So, a lot of people in the world should help each other and be kind as often they can?" At this point, I remember thinking she would go on for ever.

With patience, I replied, "Well, sometimes, we have to put ourselves first, but you see darling, the more people help each together, the better.We are all different, but a little bit of the same at the same time." She looked at me straight in the eyes, "Oh, like Noah and I both like ice cream but I prefer bubble gum ice cream and he prefers maple ice cream?" I continued to explain "Yes. A little bit like that. And a little bit like some teachers prefer to teach in schools instead of online and some musicians prefer to perform in front of a live audience." She nodded, so I went on. "Or a little bit like we all need food, but we all eat different kinds of food." I'm not sure if it all made sense to her back then.

She then asked, "Is it all bad?" I kissed her on the forehead and said "oh no, it's not all bad. Sometimes, we have to try and see beauty where it can be hard to see it." I remember her next question clearly: "And what about everything else?" I smiled at her with my eyes. "I don't know darling. What do you mean?" I replied in a light-hearted voice.

She said nothing for a minute; then added: "Are trees putting on different shoes and learning a new dance? I've never seen them this green." She didn't let me answer. "Is the sky changing into a lighter blue and taking a rest from planes? I haven't seen many fly lately, mostly birds! Is the rain making flowers prettier and giving them more colour? Are the stars and moon now sleeping underneath the clouds? I can see them much more clearly now. Are tomatoes in the garden becoming a bit shy? They became so red! And if people are helping each other, does this mean people in the world are turning into superheroes?"

I wasn't sure what to tell her, but I replied hesitantly:

"Some, yes, but not everyone is a superhero. There are always different characters in each story, but in this life, you are who you are and accept who you want to be." I said.

"Can I have more marshmallows?" She left me speechless with a smile. I paused for a while.

"Yes darling. Let's have two more each."

I thought she was done talking but then she asked, "Mum, who are your favourite superheroes?" I embraced her once more and told her, "It's you and Noah, darling."

§

I remember that night so clearly, and so does Emily. Both Noah and Emily are still my superheroes; they always will be. They taught me a lot and I am proud of them, and their Grandma had always been a great teacher to us all. Years later, Emily is now a writer and published her first book to inspire equality. Throughout the years, I suspected she'd move to London one day. Noah is now a music teacher and inspires children to learn every day. He can now play five musical instruments.

2020, It was a year when a lot of us learned about many different things, probably more than usual. No matter our differences, who we were, or who we've become, we each shared experiences, albeit in our own way.

But it was real, and it was there for all of us,
we felt it,
the feeling
of uncertainty.
Of course, there were many challenges along the way, but that
side of the story is not one for me to tell.
It was quite some time ago now, when we sat outside away from
the cherry blossom trees; we didn't light the campfire that night.

I remember that evening so clearly, when I first thought we'd only
talk about marshmallows and triple chocolate dip.

About the Author

Françoise Hélène was born in New Brunswick, Canada and lives in London, UK. After only three months of writing poetry, she won The White Label Prize. She loves developping her own philosophies and finds   inspiration through music, art, nature, spirituality and art and science research.

It is incredibly helpful if you leave a review of this book on Amazon or Goodreads and could make a difference to my career. Your thoughts and words will help me improve my work and will help me understand better my audience.

I'm grateful for every reader. Thank you so much for your support.

Join me on Instagram or Youtube

Instagram: francoisehelenepoetry
YouTube: francoisehelenepoetry

Printed in Great Britain
by Amazon

82954502R00075